Trelissick Garden

Cornwall

THE NATIONAL TRUST

Trelissick Garden

Trelissick is made by its setting: a sloping, wooded peninsula embraced by Lamouth Creek to the north, the winding estuary of the River Fal to the east, and Channal's Creek and the Carrick Roads to the south. In 1897 Hamilton Davey wrote of Trelissick as a place:

> Where no vain flowers disclosed 'a gaudy streak' but an ample range of open sward and sylvan shade, where the paths, like true Cornish lanes, wind down cool hollows and around sharp spurs at their own sweet will plunging the astonished beholder into fern fringed dell and tangled copse, where wild and cultivated flowers sweeten.

Trelissick from the air

Like many Cornish maritime gardens, Trelissick usually enjoys a mild climate and high rainfall, which enable a wide range of tender plants to be grown in the lime-free soil. But because of its high and exposed position, the garden has suffered from periodic gales (the most recent were in 1990), and also from frost and drought.

The basic framework of the woodland that shelters the garden from the Atlantic winds was planted in the 19th century. However, the special character of Trelissick only emerged in the 1930s, when Mr and Mrs Ronald Copeland began laying out a complex network of open lawns and specimen trees, broad flowerbeds and formal paths, towering shrubberies and shady dells. The planting emphasises variety of colour and scale – with red rhododendrons and blue 'lace-cap' hydrangeas providing key accents, and delicate candelabra primulas contrasting with the tall specimen conifers. All contribute to making Trelissick a real plantsman's garden.

A stand of *Rhododendron* 'Cornish Red' near the Main Lawn

The view from the Woodland Walk over the River Fal in autumn

Rhododendron macabeanum in the spring

The Development of Trelissick Garden

The River Fal from Trelissick Lawn; watercolour by R.H. Carter, 1866 (Royal Institution of Cornwall, Truro)

Ralph Allen Daniell; miniature by Henry Bone, 1795 (Royal Institution of Cornwall, Truro)

The house from the Shaded Walk

The Lawrences (by 1705–1805)
John Lawrence, a captain in the Cornwall Militia, built the first house (designed by Edmund Davey) around 1750, laid out a small park and began planting trees.

The Daniells (1805–44)
In 1805 the estate was sold to Ralph Allen Daniell, whose father, Thomas 'guinea-a-minute' Daniell, had made his fortune out of tin and copper mining in Cornwall and by marrying the heir of Ralph Allen, creator of a famous landscape garden at Prior Park, Bath (now also in the care of the National Trust). Ralph immediately set about enlarging the park by planting Carcaddon and Round Wood, and created new pleasure grounds and a kitchen garden beside the house.

His son Thomas succeeded in 1823 and two years later commissioned Peter Robinson, a pupil of the Neo-classical architect Henry Holland, to remodel the house in a severe Greek Revival style, adding a huge Ionic portico based on the Erechtheum in Athens. He also expanded the park to the north and west, and built the water tower, probably in the 1820s. Unfortunately, the cost of the new house and the mining slump of 1832 drove him into bankruptcy. He was forced to sell Trelissick to Lord Falmouth, whose great house at Tregothnan can be seen across the River Fal on the skyline (see p.13).

The Gilberts (1844–99)
After a period of uncertainty, Trelissick was bought in 1844 by John Davies Gilbert. His son Carew, who inherited in 1854, was a constant traveller, bringing back exotic trees and shrubs from North and South America, Japan and southern Europe. He planted the large Japanese Cedar (*Cryptomeria japonica*) on the main lawn, but also native species like beech, lime, sweet chestnut and elm, and many of the bigger specimen trees such as the maritime pines and the deodar and holm oaks. He built the circular rustic summer-house and created a typical late 19th-century woodland garden over 20 acres, with underplanted shrubberies of *Rhododendron ponticum*.

The Cookson and Cunliffe Era (1899–1937)
In 1899 Trelissick was let to George Cookson, who laid out a good deal of the garden, including a croquet lawn, which later became the tennis court. When he died in 1913, the estate was divided and the house and garden were let to Leonard Cunliffe, a banker, who purchased the freehold in 1928.

Trelissick rhododendrons feature on the Spode china produced by the Copeland factory

Trelissick is famous for its red rhododendrons

The Copelands (1937–55)

Cunliffe's step-daughter Ida Copeland inherited Trelissick in 1937. With her husband Ronald, she transformed the garden over the next 20 years. They introduced more hybrid rhododendrons from Lord Aberconway's famous garden at Bodnant, being particularly fond of such red-flowering varieties as 'Gwilt King' and 'Earl of Athlone', and the *Rh. griersonianum* hybrids 'Fusilier', 'Tally Ho' and 'May Day'. Many appear on the Spode china produced by W.T. Copeland & Sons Ltd, of which Ronald Copeland was managing director. The Copelands also planted many camellias and white-flowering Japanese cherries, which had become popular in the 1940s.

In 1955 Mrs Copeland generously gave 376 acres of garden, park and woodland to the National Trust. The mansion remains the family home, where a collection of Copeland and Spode china is shown to visitors by prior appointment twice a year. The family name is perpetuated in the garden through the daffodils 'Irene Copeland' and 'Mary Copeland', which can be seen in the Dell each spring.

The National Trust

The National Trust has now looked after Trelissick since 1955. Gardens never stand still, and because of the recent storm damage, substantial new planting has been essential. The Trust has thickened the protective shelter belt of woodland, and introduced more rhododendrons, hydrangeas and maples, replacing frost-damaged tender evergreens. The Hydrangea Walk, Fern Garden and Scented Garden have been developed with plants chosen that will extend the flowering season beyond the traditional spring flourish.

In 1937 Ronald Copeland developed the western half of Carcaddon, the area to the north of the road to King Harry Ferry, by planting numerous rhododendrons, camellias and cherries. The eastern half was originally an orchard, which became overgrown during the Second World War. In the 1960s the then head gardener, Jack Lilly, with the help of the Trust's Gardens Adviser, Graham Stuart Thomas, redesigned Carcaddon as an informal garden of exotic trees and flowering shrubs, divided by lawns and covered with carpets of bulbs in spring. In 1897 F.Hamilton Davey described Trelissick as 'the fruit garden of Cornwall', and in 1995 the Trust re-established two acres of orchard with old Cornish varieties of apple.

Ferris's Cottage in spring

Tour of the Garden

The Water Tower

The Water Tower (B)

The conical twin roofs of the water tower have become the emblem of Trelissick. The building was put up, probably in the 1820s, by Thomas Daniell, in order to provide water pressure for the house and garden in their elevated position. Carew Gilbert added the squirrel weathervane from his family coat of arms in the late 19th century. The tower is now rented out as one of five holiday cottages at Trelissick.

The Stables (2)

These were built in the early 19th century, when the parkland rides were being developed. The Copeland horse appears on the weathervane. The harness and tack rooms contain a magnificent collection of carriage and heavy horse harness and other equipment. There is also a small exhibition devoted to the history of the estate in the Ladder Walk. (The stable yard is not open.)

The Fig Garden (3)

This triangular bed, to the right of the entrance path, was filled with Brown Turkey figs until they were destroyed by frosts of $-15\,^{\circ}$C in 1979. Eleven different cultivars have been replanted, and the shady, north-facing wall behind is covered with ivies.

The Scented Garden (4)

The warmer bed on the left was originally used for growing early vegetables, flowers and herbs for the house. The garden is now planted with a collection of plants selected for their fragrance and texture, with visitors with sensory impairments in mind.

The Entrance Walk (6)

This border is backed by the south-facing wall of the old kitchen garden. In spring it features old Chinese and Japanese wisterias, arabis and Copeland tulips, and *Viburnum × juddii*, with its distinctive scent of cloves. They are followed in summer by warm-coloured *Canna iridiflora*, dahlias, old fragrant varieties of heliotrope (a special favourite of Ida Copeland), the scented *Trachelospermum jasminoïdes* and the large, late-flowering *Clematis flammula*. Opposite is a small fern garden, which features a statue of a Piping Boy, given by Mr and Mrs Spencer Copeland to commemorate the centenary of the National Trust in 1995.

Wisteria in flower at the entrance to the garden

View from the Tennis Lawn

The view over the river from the Celtic Cross

The Main Lawn (7)

A big clump of *Rhododendron* 'Cornish Red' stands on one side of the entrance to this area. Sloping away from you is the broad lawn – an unusual feature for a Cornish garden – and the eye is carried to the trees and shrubs on the far slope known as Carcaddon (16). The lawn is dominated by the spreading branches of the *Cryptomeria japonica* planted by Carew Gilbert in 1898. The deep mixed borders that surround the lawn contain a wide range of trees, shrubs and herbaceous plants, designed to create interest throughout the year. The border, backed by the high wall of the kitchen garden, is mainly confined to soft colours, while that near the sunken road, facing south, contains bolder shades.

The Shaded Walk (8)

The paths to the right of the lawn lead into the old part of the garden east of the house. At the first crossroads summer-flowering shrubs dominate: groups of hydrangeas, hebes, cistus, hypericum and the autumn-flowering eupatorium. Here is the first view of the mansion with a granite memorial stone dedicated to Ronald and Ida Copeland. The bottle oven symbol recalls the Copeland china factory, the Scout fleur-de-lis Mr Copeland's involvement in the movement. Mrs Copeland was an MP and District Commissioner for Guides: hence the Houses of Parliament and the Guide trefoil.

The Shaded Walk is at its best in early spring with daffodils, crocuses and hellebores mingling with wild flowers. Camellias, rhododendrons and mahonias provide colour under the trees.

The Tennis Lawn (9)

The rustic Victorian summer-house overlooks a former tennis court which commands magnificent views of the Carrick Roads, stretching out towards Falmouth. The view was enhanced when the Trust removed a park fence and constructed a ha-ha. The shrubs that surround the tennis court are selected for their tolerance of salt winds: escallonias, olearias, *Rhododendron ponticum*, *Bupleurum fruticosum*, phormiums and kniphofias. In this area is also the Cornish 'Menhyr' stone that was set up to mark the millennium.

The Celtic Cross (10)

Legend has it that from here the local priest preached to the fishermen in their boats below, the acoustics being especially good.

The Japanese Cedar (*Cryptomeria japonica*) in the middle of the Main Lawn was planted in 1898

Ferris's Cottage from the Dell

Ferns flank this path through the garden

The Tregothnan View (11)

The curved seat commands a view of Tregothnan, the home of Viscount Falmouth, which can be seen on the skyline. This part of the garden faces north, and so suffers less from early morning sun damaging frosted blooms of the camellias and rhododendrons for which the garden is renowned. Look out here for white hydrangeas, eucryphias and orange kniphofias.

The Woodland Paths (12)

The visitor often overlooks these paths, which lead to some unusual rhododendrons and camellias, with underplantings of cyclamen, erythronium, anemone, maianthemum, primroses and foxgloves, mingling with native wild flowers.

The Hydrangea Walk (13)

The theme of hydrangeas overhung with flowering cherries created by the Copelands has been retained, complemented by evergreen spindles and a fine *Halesia carolina* (Snowdrop tree). In spring the grassy banks are covered with narcissi, *Pseudo-narcissus* 'Princeps' and the old 'Barrii' varieties, and several rhododendrons give added interest at this season. Glimpses of the River Fal and the King Harry Ferry can be enjoyed from here.

The Dell (14)

This area is at its most beautiful in late spring and summer. The large-leaved rhododendrons such as the white *johnstoneanum* and brilliant yellow 'Mary Swaythling' are underplanted with astilbes, filipendulas, rodgersias, ferns and candelabra primulas. The higher banks are left to wild flowers and daffodils, while the lower, bog garden is dominated by *Gunnera maincata* and Himalayan bamboo, with hostas, skunk lily and Himalayan cowslip. The daffodils 'Irene Copeland' and 'Mary Copeland' were propagated by Ronald Copeland's brother William and are named after his daughters. The Australian tree ferns (*Dicksonia antarctica*) give a tropical flavour to this part of the garden.

View of the rustic bridge through the Dell

Carcaddon in May

The Bridge (15)

The rustic bridge, which connects the two parts of the garden, crosses the road to King Harry Ferry (20). The road itself is seen only from the bridge and from most parts of the garden is hidden from view. The bridge is a recent replacement in wood of a brick and concrete structure, its rustic design reflecting the thatched summer-house in Carcaddon.

Carcaddon (16)

The Cornish prefix 'Car' or 'Caer' denotes a fortified place. The eastern end of Carcaddon was brought into the garden proper in the early 1960s, having previously been an old orchard and nursery. It is now beginning to establish itself and contains mass plantings of daffodils followed by camellias, magnolias (including *M.* 'Trelissick'), rhododendrons, viburnum and many other shrubs. Deutzia gives an early summer show, and 'lace-cap' hydrangeas offer colour well into the autumn. The latter are a particular feature of Trelissick, with more than 150 kinds being grown. Hydrangeas and hybrid rhododendrons were extensively planted by Ronald Copeland before the Second World War, and the range has been extended by the National Trust. Beyond is the recently planted wild flower meadow, which is interspersed with Cornish daffodils and apple trees.

The Park (18)

The parkland forms an integral part of the estate and is a perfect foreground to the views of the Carrick Roads. Separated from the garden by a ha-ha, it is a fine example of the English landscape style. A booklet describes riverside walks through the woodland to Lamouth Creek and Roundwood Quay.

The rustic bridge

The summer-house in Carcaddon